D1398011

THE
STANLEY
CUP

Jonathan Bliss

HOCKEY

HEROES

Rourke Book Company, Inc.
Vero Beach, Florida 32964

The Rourke Book Co., Inc.
P.O. Box 3328, Vero Beach, FL 32964

Bliss, Jonathan.
   The Stanley Cup / Jonathan Bliss.
      p. cm. — (Hockey heroes)
   Includes bibliographical references (p. 47) and index.
   ISBN 1-55916-012-8
   1. Stanley Cup (Hockey)—History—Juvenile literature.
   2. Montreal Canadiens (Hockey team)—Juvenile literature.
   3. National Hockey League—Juvenile literature. [1. Stanley Cup
   (Hockey)—History. 2. Hockey—History.] I. Title. II. Series.
   GV847.7.B54 1994
   796.962'648—dc20   93-50579
                                                                CIP
                                                                 AC

Series Editor: Gregory Lee
Book design and production: The Creative Spark, San Clemente, CA
Cover photograph: ALLSPORT

Printed in the USA

Contents

The excitement of hockey is reaching more fans today than in its first 100 years. Action at high speed is the thrilling ingredient in today's hockey.

To Be the Best

Two men in bulky pads and painted masks crouch in front of their nets, 190 feet apart. Between them skate ten players wielding curved sticks in an unfriendly way—12 men in an area 85 feet wide by 200 feet long fighting for possession of a tiny, hard rubber disc. Things happen too fast in hockey for conscious decisions. There is no time to run set plays like there is in football or baseball, and there is no time to consider your next move as in basketball. The fan sees only a blur of activity. A stick slams into the puck, sending it careening toward a goalie at 120 miles per hour. A body slams into another body which slams into the rink wall, dissolving in a tangle of sticks, fists, and skates.

Stanley Cup Trivia

Q: How was the first Stanley Cup decided?
A: It was a two-game showdown, with the team scoring the most total goals taking the prize.

Q: The Stanley Cup has been cancelled only once in its history. When and why?
A: The 1918-19 final between Montreal and Seattle was cancelled after five games due to a worldwide influenza epidemic. The legendary Joe Malone died as a result.

A good hockey team must win more games than they lose, keep their losing streaks to a minimum, and play hard every night. These are the contenders for the division crowns. To be a consistent winner, each player must raise their game a notch for the playoffs. To be a Stanley Cup-winning team, a franchise must have the talent and the dedication to survive other equally skilled teams—clubs must battle through three best-of-seven series against increasingly difficult opponents before reaching the best-of-seven finals. That's a minimum of 16 games. Question: How difficult is this feat? Answer: Fifteen of the 26 clubs in the modern NHL have never won a Stanley Cup. There are no weaklings in the Stanley Cup finals.

And what makes a dynasty? Only teams that can put together year after year of serious Stanley Cup play. This book describes those few teams in hockey history who were better than good. Here are the greatest hockey teams of all time.

The Early Years

The idea of hitting an object with a stick has been around since ancient times. The native Americans of North America played a game called lacrosse which involved two goals, catching sticks, and a soft ball. An early version of stick ball played on ice was called "shinny"—basically a game of keep away using various sticks and balls.

The earliest reported hockey game was on March 3, 1875 when the *Montreal Gazette* described a series of games involving two nine-men teams. The competition ended in a brawl, including both players and spectators! The final game was cancelled. Other accounts credit W.F. Robertson, "Chick" Murray, and Dick Smith with creating the game of hockey to keep a football team in shape during the off-season.

The man whose name graces professional hockey's greatest prize was Lord Stanley of Preston, an official of the Canadian government.

The first rules were a blend of rugby, lacrosse, and skating. There is no telling which story is true; perhaps both are.

By 1883, hockey was a regular feature in the Montreal Winter Carnival. Teams competed from Toronto, Ottawa, Quebec, and Montreal. In time, hockey leagues became numerous, and spectators began to see the first recognizable stars. In 1893, several leagues agreed to hold a playoff to determine a world champion. Canada's Governor General, Lord Stanley of Preston, would award the prize—a trophy which became known as the Stanley Cup.

The Two Victorias

The first two teams to dominate the Stanley Cup were both named the Victorias. The Montreal Victorias won the Stanley Cup in 1894. The team roster included future Hall-of-Famers Mike Grant and Graham Drinkwater. The Montreal Vics were unseated by the Winnipeg Victorias the following year. Winnipeg was led by Dan Bain and George Merrit, one of the greatest goaltenders of all time. Merrit had the distinction of being the first goalie to wear protective gear, using his cricket pads to ward off serious injury.

The Montreal Vics went west to Winnipeg the next year to reclaim the Cup. Winnipeg fans paid up to $12 a

*The first Stanley Cup champions were
the 1898 Montreal Victorias.*

seat (the equivalent of $150 today) to see their heroes play. In Montreal, in a preview of the live sports events we enjoy on television, telegraph operators sent play-by-play descriptions of the games, and the streets of Montreal were mobbed by fans awaiting news. Montreal prevailed, bringing the Cup back east.

The Ottawa Silver Seven

Hockey's original dynasty became the first team to win the Stanley Cup three years in a row. The Ottawa Silver Seven boasted a powerful lineup which included Frank McGee, the three Gilmour brothers (David, Billy, and Suddy), Alf and Harry Smith, and Harry Westwick.

Perhaps the best known of Ottawa's defenses of the Cup was with Dawson City. It took the Dawson City team 23 days to reach Ottawa by dog sled, boat, and train, traveling 4,400 miles. It was a long way to come, only to be beaten by scores of 9-2 and 23-2! Ottawa's one-eyed Frank McGee scored a Cup record 14 goals in the second game.

The Silver Seven were virtually unbeatable until the spring of 1906 when they gave up the Cup to the Montreal Wanderers in a two-game series. The Silver Seven didn't give the Cup up without a fight—literally. After a heated argument, the Stanley Cup was almost thrown into Ontario's Lake of the Woods. This wasn't the first time the Cup was nearly lost. A player once booted it into a canal (luckily the canal was frozen solid and the Cup was recovered).

The Montreal Wanderers

The Wanderers was perhaps the last championship hockey team that was more amateur than professional. It featured such players as Ernie Russell, Lester Patrick, Riley Hern, Ernie Johnstone, and Hod Stuart. Known as the "Redbands" for the red stripe on their jerseys, the Wanderers were top notch. The 1907 series included more future Hall-of-Famers than any other contest, when Montreal was beaten by the Kenora Thistles. However, the Wanderers reclaimed the trophy and held it through 1908. The next year it was claimed by the heir to the Silver Seven crown, the Ottawa Senators.

The Ottawa Senators

Ottawa won their first Stanley Cup in 1909 and came back a year later to win it again in 1910-11. In 1919-20, the Senators put up the best figures overall in the NHL, winning both halves of the NHL's split schedule (19 wins, 5 losses). The Senators sported an amazing crew, including centerman Frank Nighbor,

Frank Nighbor was a standout center for the champion Ottawa Senators of Canada.

defenseman Sprague Cleghorn, and goalie Clint Benedict. Benedict had recorded a record five shutouts in a 24-game season. Ottawa won two years straight.

Toronto managed to unseat Ottawa the following year, but in 1922-23 the Senators returned, finishing first in the regular season standings with 14-9. The Senators blanked the Canadiens for the Cup. During the first game, Montreal's Sprague Cleghorn (newly acquired from Ottawa) and Billy Couture played viciously, injuring several Ottawa stars with their sticks and elbows. Although undermanned due to the injuries, the Senators won their third Cup in four years.

Ottawa won once more in 1926-27, taking the series against Boston. On that last great Senator team, eight of the twelve players would eventually end up in the Hockey Hall of Fame.

By 1930, the Great Depression had the Senators by the throat. The Senators won only 10 games in the 1930-31 season, finished last in the standings, and requested a one-year leave of absence from the league. The Senators returned for the 1932-33 season, but could manage only two more years as bottom dwellers before moving to St. Louis to become the Eagles. It would be almost 60 years before the Senators rejoined the NHL.

*Maple Leafs owner Conn Smythe was one of the architects of the
National Hockey League. His Toronto team became one of the "solid
six"—the only teams to rule the early NHL of the 1940s and '50s.*

The Era of the Solid Six

The 1925-26 season marked the last time the Stanley Cup was contested between two leagues. The NHL's original rival, the PCHA, went bankrupt, and other leagues met the same fate. This left the NHL as the dominant hockey league, and made the Stanley Cup playoffs the popular prize. In 1926-27, the NHL divided into two divisions, the Canadian Division and the American Division. Six teams made the playoffs under this new format, and three series were played to determine the Stanley Cup winner, with the final series being a best-of-seven games.

Unfortunately, the Great Depression worsened and many clubs dropped out, reducing the number of teams from eight in two divisions to a single seven-team league (1938-39). At the end of the 1941-42 season, the NHL shrank to just six teams. These were the Solid Six: Toronto, Montreal, New York, Boston, Detroit, and Chicago. For the next 25 years, these teams would fight it out for the Cup. The same teams met each other in the finals over and over again. This was an age of conservative hockey played by a small number of gifted hockey players. Out of this era came some of the great dynasties in hockey history.

The Toronto Maple Leafs: 1944-51

During their greatest years the Toronto Maple Leafs never finished first in the regular season except once. They always saved their best hockey for the playoffs. Their success was created by owner Conn Smythe and talent scout Frank Selke, who brought the right personnel to the Maple Leafs. Coach Hap Day paced his team so that it would peak at just the right moment.

The first glimpse of the Maple Leafs dynasty came in the 1942 playoffs. Toronto finished second that year behind the New York Rangers, who had three of the top four scorers in the league. But the Maple Leafs also had a star-studded cast, including Syl Apps, Sweeney Schriner, Gordie Drillon, and standout goalie Turk Broda. Toronto eliminated the Rangers in the opening round of the playoffs, leading to a final-round matchup with the Red Wings. Detroit stunned the Leafs by winning the first three games (two of them in Toronto). Toronto's Billy Taylor joked after the third game that the Maple Leafs were just warming up. But could Toronto come back from a three-game deficit? Conn Smythe and Hap Day shook up the Toronto lineup, putting in seldom-used forwards Don Metz and Ernie Dickens. The Metz-Dickens combination clicked, providing Toronto with three straight wins to tie up the series. In the seventh game, Sweeney Schriner scored two goals to win the decisive game and the Cup. Billy Taylor was right.

It would be three more seasons before Toronto made the finals again. They finished the regular season with a mediocre 24-22-4 record, while the Montreal Canadiens lost only eight games all season. The Canadiens were coming off a Cup-winning season and were favored to repeat, especially with Elmer Lach, Maurice Richard and Toe Blake finishing one-two-three in scoring. But Toronto stung Montreal with two quick victories in the opening round behind rookie goaltender Frank McCool. Toronto eliminated the Canadiens in six games, setting the stage for a duel with Gordie Howe and the Detroit Red Wings.

Forward Don Metz proved to be a breath of fresh air in Toronto's lineup, spearheading a come-from-behind victory in the 1942 Stanley Cup Championship.

Detroit nearly erased the memory of their embarrassing Cup loss three years before by turning history on its head. This time it was Toronto that won the first three games—all of them shutouts by goalie Frank McCool—before Detroit staged a comeback, winning the next three games. The seventh game looked to be Detroit's, but defenseman Babe Pratt's dramatic goal in the third period stung the Red Wings, and the Maple Leafs became champions again.

The next season, Smythe and Selke let some older players go and brought up rookies like Bill Barilko, Bill Ezinicki, and Howie Meeker. The core of the team—Syl Apps, Don and Nick Metz, and Ted Kennedy—remained. And the Cup of 1945-46 remained in Toronto.

Toronto increased the strength on its front line next by trading five players to Chicago for top goal scorer Max Bentley. Not only did the Leafs win the regular season title in 1947-48, they also swept through the playoffs, meeting the Detroit Red Wings in the finals. Goalie Turk Broda shut down the Red Wings' Production Line, and the Maple Leafs triumphed in four straight games. The next season, Toronto took its third Cup in a row.

After losing the Stanley Cup to Detroit in the 1949-50 season, Toronto came back for its fourth Cup in five years. Turk Broda's goals-against average had dropped each year from 2.24 in 1947 to a stunning 1.12 in 1951. The victim this time was Montreal, as Toronto swept to the Cup in five games. In the fifth and deciding game, Toronto trailed 2-1 in the final period before coach Joe Primeau yanked goalie Broda for an extra attacker. The maneuver paid off as Tod Sloan put home the game-tying goal with just 32 seconds left in regulation. Less than three minutes into overtime, defenseman Bill Barilko won the game and the Cup for the Leafs. It was the last goal Barilko would ever score; he lost his life in a plane crash a few weeks after that game.

The Red Wings "Production Line" offense consisted of (from l to r) Gordie Howe, Sid Abel, and Ted Lindsay. They were a potent force in the NHL for much of the 1950s.

The Detroit Red Wings: 1947-57

If the Toronto team of the late 1940s was a team that won without superstars, the Detroit Red Wings were just the opposite, a team that was filled with talent, including one of the greatest hockey players of all time, Gordie Howe. Howe did everything well: He was not only the NHL's top scorer, he was also the league's fastest, strongest, smoothest-skating, and, on occasion, meanest player. Howe was one-third of the formidable Production Line offense. With the Production Line, the Red Wings finished second in 1947-48, then recorded an unprecedented seven consecutive first-place finishes and four Stanley Cups in the decade that followed.

Besides a potent offense, Detroit also had the best defenseman in future Hall of Famer Leonard "Red" Kelly, a two-way hockey player. Goalies Harry Lumley and Terry Sawchuk were also key; Sawchuk is the only goalie in NHL history to register more than 100 shutouts. And General Manager Jack Adams (who had coached the team between 1927 and 1947) contributed to their success by developing the first effective farm system for grooming young talent.

From 1942 to 1949, Detroit generally finished either first or second in the regular season. In 1950, the Red Wings were ready for greatness, but their first playoff opponent was Toronto. That was bad news for the Red Wings, who had dropped 11 straight playoff games to the Maple Leafs in the past three years. In the opening game of the series, Toronto's Ted Kennedy sidestepped a Howe check and the Detroit star went head-first into the boards. Howe almost died that night in a hospital as surgeons worked to relieve pressure on his brain. Fortunately, he recovered to play the following season.

Without their great right winger, the Red Wings lost that first game, 5-0, and things looked bleak. But Detroit fought back and defeated the Maple Leafs in seven games. In the finals, the Red Wings met the New York Rangers and trailed them three games to two. In the sixth game, the Rangers led 4-3 going into the third period before Ted Lindsay and Sid Abel saved the day and tied up the series. The seventh game was tied in the third period when, as so often happens, the game and the Cup were decided by a relative unknown. In overtime, Red Wing forward Pete Babando scored, delivering the Cup to Detroit.

During the 1950-51 season, Gordie Howe dominated the scoring charts with 43 goals and 43 assists to finish 20 points ahead of Maurice Richard. Terry Sawchuk's season was equally dominating as he took the Vezina Trophy with 12 shutouts. Toronto was toast again as Bill Barilko's stirring overtime goal in the fifth and deciding game gave Detroit the victory. The next year, Detroit steamrolled over Montreal in four straight games, and the dynasty seemed set. But then Detroit ran into a goalie even hotter than Sawchuk in the semifinals: Boston's Sugar Jim Henry. Henry was too good for the Production Line, and the Bruins won the Cup in six games.

In 1953-54, the Red Wings needed just five games to eliminate Toronto, while Montreal took Boston in four to set up one of the greatest series in Stanley Cup history. The Production Line devastated the Canadiens and goalie Jacques Plante by winning three of the first four games. Then Canadiens' coach Dick Irvin replaced Plante, recalling 31-year-old Gerry McNeil from the minors. McNeil shut out the Red Wings in the fifth game, with Montreal winning in overtime. Then the Canadiens evened the series at three games apiece.

The seventh game went into overtime, tied at 1-1. With four-and-a-half minutes gone, Detroit's Tony Leswick lifted a puck toward McNeil. Canadien defenseman Doug Harvey lifted his glove to block the shot. Instead, Harvey's glove deflected the puck past McNeil's shoulder and into the Montreal net, giving Detroit the Stanley Cup.

The next year was the last year of the Detroit dynasty. Montreal was coming on strong. It was fitting that the two teams should meet in the finals, where Montreal took the series to 3-3 before the Red Wings, with home ice advantage, finally won. It would be Detroit's last Stanley Cup. The dynastic crown would soon go to Montreal.

Toronto Maple Leafs II: 1961-67

Since their glory years in the 1940s, the Maple Leafs had done badly. By 1957, Toronto had hit bottom and owner Conn Smythe decided it was time for a change. He

Frank Mahovlich of Toronto (white jersey) goes one-on-one with Rangers goalie Ed Giacomin.

hired George "Punch" Imlach as the Leafs' General Manager. Imlach made himself coach. He acquired Bert Olmstead from the Canadiens and picked up journeyman goalie Johnny Bower. The result was a respectable fourth place finish and a spot in the playoffs. They proceeded to shock second-place Boston before meeting and losing decisively to Montreal in the finals. The Leafs kept returning to the playoffs year after year, but were always denied.

Finally, the scorers began to emerge. Frank Mahovlich finished the 1960-61 season third on the scoring list behind Bernie Geoffrion and Jean Beliveau. Red Kelly, the consummate playmaker for the Leafs, was also up on the scoring list with Dave Keon and Bob Pulford, always good for 20 goals a year. The 1961-62 season proceeded as many past seasons had, with the Montreal machine winning their fifth straight title, but Toronto hung tough. Once again, the Hawks' tough checking unhinged the Canadiens and Chicago won it in six with Stan Mikita and Bobby Hull starring. This left the door wide open for Toronto, who had eliminated the New York Rangers, winning the pivotal fifth game in double overtime on Red Kelly's goal—despite a superb performance by Gump Worsley, who stopped 56 shots. The Leafs went on to win the Stanley Cup from Chicago in six games, sparked by Bob Pulford's three-goal performance in a fifth game romp, 8-4.

In 1962-63, Punch Imlach went out and got Kent Douglas, a young defenseman. Douglas fit in immediately, winning the Calder Trophy as the league's top rookie, leading the Leafs to the championship by a single point over Chicago and three points over Montreal. In the playoffs, Toronto once again prevailed, beating the Canadiens in five games, then taking Detroit in five. Imlach pulled off another major trade in 1963-64 when he got Andy Bathgate and Don McKenney from New York. Together, these two men gave Toronto just enough fire power to survive the playoffs, taking down Montreal in seven games, then stretching to the limit to beat Detroit in seven more for their third straight Cup.

After losing to Montreal the following two seasons, Toronto came storming back in 1966-67. They finished a distant third in the regular season, but in the playoffs the Maple Leafs slid past Chicago in six games, then defeated Montreal in six for their eleventh Stanley Cup. That made it four Cups in five years.

Toe Blake, who played outstanding offense for the Canadiens during the 1940s, became Montreal's coach for its dominating Stanley Cup success of the 1950s.

The Montreal Canadiens

There has never been a team in all of hockey—no, all of professional sports—like the Montreal Canadiens. No team in the NHL has won more Stanley Cups than Montreal. So thoroughly have the Canadiens dominated the sport that by the end of the 1993 season Montreal had won 24 of the 100 Cups contested.

The Canadiens' dynasty can be divided roughly into two great periods. There had been other strong Montreal teams before the 1950s—the franchise already owned six Stanley Cups by then—but the Montreal team of the 1950s was perhaps the greatest team in hockey history.

The First Dynasty: 1952-1960

In 1946-47, Frank Selke (the same genius behind the Maple Leafs' dynasty) had been

Stanley Cup Trivia

Q: Which team holds the record for the most power play goals in one season?
A: Pittsburgh, with 120 (1988-89).

Q: Which team had the highest goals-per-game average in NHL history?
A: Edmonton, with 5.58 (1983-84).

Q: Which team has won the most Stanley Cups?
A: The Montreal Canadiens, with 24 championships.

lured away from Toronto to become the General Manager for the Canadiens. Under his guidance, the Canadiens slowly added talent to their lineup. The most important addition was Jean Beliveau, a tall young center from Quebec. Montreal didn't get him cheap—in fact, the Canadiens had to purchase an entire amateur league just to get him. When Beliveau was finally put in the 1954-55 lineup, the team was ready to make history.

At the team's core was the fiery centerman Maurice Richard, one of the greatest players of all times. Beside him were other marksmen like Bernie "Boom Boom" Geoffrion, Bert Olmstead, and Dickie Moore. Doug Harvey, a defensive legend, anchored a rock solid defense while goalie Jacques Plante stood "between the pipes."

New coach and former Punch Line member Toe Blake added three rookies to the team: Henri Richard (younger brother of Maurice), defenseman Jean Guy Talbot, and forward Claude Provost. This edition of the Montreal Canadiens romped over the opposition, going 45-15-10 and winning the league championship by 24 points. Four of the six first-team selections to the All-Star game were Canadiens: Maurice Richard, Beliveau, Harvey, and Plante. Post-season honors were also a family affair: Plante won the Vezina for best goalie, Harvey took the Norris for top defenseman, and Beliveau received the Hart Trophy for the league's MVP. Montreal beat Detroit in the Stanley Cup finals, defeating them in five games for their first Cup in more than a decade.

The 1956-57 season saw Coach Toe Blake working hard to perfect the Montreal power play, with Geoffrion and Harvey at the points, Richard at right wing, Beliveau at center, and either Moore or Olmstead at left wing. The effect was awe-inspiring. The Canadiens could score two or three goals on a single penalty (until the NHL changed the penalty rule).

*The Montreal Canadiens had an overabundance of talented
players, such as "Boom Boom" Geoffrion.*

Montreal eliminated New York in five games during the semifinals, then bowled over the Boston Bruins. Richard set the tone by scoring four goals in a 5-1 opener as Montreal took the Cup in five games.

Andre Provonost and Maurice Richard suffered major injuries during the 1957-58 season, yet the team still finished first. Richard returned just in time to drive the Canadiens through to the Stanley Cup, sweeping by Detroit in four straight, then taking Boston in six as Richard contributed 11 goals in 10 playoff games. The next year (1958-59), Montreal won it all again despite Bert Olmstead being traded to Toronto and Maurice ("The Rocket") Richard out of the playoffs with a broken ankle. Once again, Moore, Geoffrion, and Beliveau supplied the firepower, and Plante (who collected his fourth Vezina Trophy) supplied the brick wall, as Montreal eliminated Boston in five games to take their unprecedented fourth Stanley Cup in a row.

Would 1958-59 be any different? Yes: Plante took to wearing a mask. Montreal beat Toronto by 13 points for the regular season title, then eliminated Chicago and Toronto in four games each to win their fifth consecutive title—an all-time Stanley Cup record.

The Canadiens' golden era ended in 1960 when Maurice Richard retired. After 18 seasons in professional hockey and 544 goals, he was off the ice. While all of Quebec mourned, the rest of the NHL celebrated. The Canadiens still managed to capture their fourth straight regular-season championship, beating out Toronto by an unexpectedly thin margin of two points. Everyone anticipated another Canadiens victory in the Stanley Cup, but the Black Hawks intimidated Montreal with tough bodychecking and got consecutive shutouts from goalie Glenn Hall to beat Montreal and end their great run. No one else would ever do it again.

The swift Yvan Cournoyer (number 12) contributed to the second great Canadien dynasty of the 1970s, one of the greatest teams in history.

The Second Dynasty: 1964-79

What more could fans expect from a team that won five Stanley Cups in a row? How about another decade of domination? By the mid-1960s, the Canadiens were at it again. While The Rocket was gone, his brother Henri was still around and fast as ever. So was Jean Beliveau and Claude Provost. More speed joined the club in the person of Yvan Cournoyer, "The Roadrunner." He was undoubtedly the fastest player in the league. On defense, the Canadiens were led by Jacques Laperriere, rookie of the year in 1964.

More than just individual players, Montreal had a winning tradition on its side. The locker room contained photographs of former greats; the banners of past Stanley Cups hung down over the Forum ice. If you were a Canadien, you were confident that history was on your side. All Montreal teams seemed modeled on the same winning principles: strong defense, great speed, and stylish teamwork.

Montreal had one weakness: They were a small team, and when they were pounded, they could be beaten. That was until they started to get enforcers like John Ferguson on their team, who protected the smaller guys. In 1964-65, both Toronto and Chicago tried to beat up on Montreal and failed. The next year, Montreal did it again. After a penalty-marred battle against the Leafs which ended in a Canadien sweep, they took on Detroit. The Red Wings won the first two games of the series, but the Canadiens roared back to win four straight and claim their second consecutive Cup.

The expansion of the NHL in 1967 had little effect on Montreal. If anything, it made them a stronger team. They dominated the East Division, winning yet another championship. In the playoffs, Montreal breezed past Boston, took the Black Hawks in five, then swept St. Louis in four. Twice the expansion Blues forced games into overtime, but both times the Canadiens prevailed. In the 1968-69 season, they beat the emerging Boston superpower in six games (including three overtime games) before crushing St. Louis once again for their sixteenth Stanley Cup—four trophies in five years.

When Montreal failed to make the playoffs in 1969-70 (the first time in 22 years), the team added Guy Lafleur, a superstar forward, and goalie Ken Dryden. Dryden almost singlehandedly stopped the powerful Boston offense cold. Montreal eliminated Boston in seven games—a stunning upset—and then advanced to knock off Minnesota and Chicago.

After being bludgeoned by Boston in 1971-72,

*Ken Dryden was one of the greatest goalies in NHL history,
which made the Montreal Canadiens of the 1970s one of the
greatest teams in history.*

Montreal reinforced its ranks with a trio of great players—one old favorite and two future stars. The old favorite was former Maple Leaf Frank Mahovlich. The kids were defenseman Larry Robinson and left winger Steve Shutt. Suddenly, Montreal had a team that was almost too good to beat. They certainly played that way, losing only 10 games and tying 16 in a 78-game schedule. The Canadiens dismantled Chicago in six games for the Cup.

There was a brief pause while the Philadelphia Flyers bullied their way to the Stanley Cup, pushing their weight around more than pushing the puck around. Could strong, aggressive play outscore speed and style? Slender, graceful Guy Lafleur supplied the answer. In 1975-76, the Canadiens finished the season with 58 victories and 127 points (both records). They led the league in virtually every category, and they did it all with the lowest penalty-minute totals in the league. In the playoffs they won 12 out of 13 games, including a sweep of Philadelphia in the finals. Lafleur, who had won the scoring title with 125 points, had 17 points in the playoffs.

In the 1976-77 season, Montreal's domination was so complete that four of the six members of the All-Star first team were Canadiens (Robinson, Shutt, Lafleur, and Dryden). The Canadiens won 60 games, lost only eight, and set a new record with a total of 132 points—20 points ahead of their nearest challenger. In their own arena, the Montreal Forum, the Canadiens lost only once in 40 games, tying the modern NHL record for fewest home losses. To no one's surprise, Montreal took most of the post-season honors (Lafleur with the Art Ross, the Hart, and the Conn Smythe; Dryden with the Vezina; and Robinson with the Norris) and won the Stanley Cup convincingly, sweeping the Bruins in the finals.

The Bruins were outmatched the very next season,

managing only two wins before succumbing to the Canadiens' overwhelming play; Montreal allowed the Bruins only 12 goals in six games. Once again, the post-season awards went to Canadiens and once again, it was their due. In 1978-79, Montreal won its fourth straight Cup, derailing the Rangers in the finals, 4-1, as Bob Gainey, yet another Canadien standout, won the Conn Smythe as playoff MVP. At the end of the 1979 season, Ken Dryden retired from hockey. With his departure went the element that had made Montreal unbeatable over the last half dozen years. Now, they were merely a great team.

The NHL is a much larger league than it was 50 years ago. New stars such as Pavel Bure are on their way to joining the legends of the past.

The Expanding League

When the NHL decided to expand in 1967, it changed many things. In a span of 11 years, the league grew from six to 18 teams. The arrangement brought many new fans into the sport. It also brought a lot of new players into the league. Some of these players were undiscovered stars. Many others were just average—players who might never have made it into a smaller, six-team league. The more-talented players had an easier time scoring. Fifty goals per season was no longer out of reach for top-flight players. The established clubs feasted on the expansion clubs. In the first year of the new arrangement, the East Division (which featured the original Solid Six) romped over the expansion teams clustered in the West Division.

Eventually, teams that hobbled through their first two or three seasons would become dynasties, competing on an equal footing with Montreal or Toronto. And one team that had hibernated for decades woke up one day to find itself perched on hockey greatness: the Boston Bruins.

The Boston Bruins: 1970-1973

Throughout most of their history, the Bruins had been a mediocre team. Except for the Eddie Shore years during the late 1930s and early 1940s (when the Bruins actually won two Stanley Cups in three years), Boston rarely managed even a playoff berth. That all changed

One of the most famous moments in Stanley Cup history occurred when Boston's Bobby Orr tipped in the winning goal in overtime to take the championship over the St. Louis Blues.

in the early 1970s when Boston combined role players and genuine superstars into a cohesive working team.

In 1969-70, Bobby Orr simply destroyed every record for scoring by a defenseman: 33 goals, 87 assists, and 120 points. He became the first defenseman in history to win the scoring title, only the fourth player ever to go over 100 points (just six points short of Esposito's record of the year before). In the playoffs, Boston steamed through New York, Chicago, and St. Louis, winning the last 10 games in a row. The Stanley Cup-winning goal came in overtime of the Bruins' fourth game against St. Louis. Bobby Orr came streaking in alone and broke through a line of Blues defenders before St. Louis' Noel Picard upended him.

In mid-air, while falling to the ice, Orr managed to wrist a shot past Blues goalie Glenn Hall for the winner.

In 1970-71, Boston was king of the league. Esposito and Orr were the scoring kings, and four other Bruins were also among the league's top 10 scorers. Boston finished with a record 399 goals for the season, an average of more than five goals per game. It was no wonder that Boston took the East championship, losing only 14 games all season. But their offense couldn't get past Montreal's rookie goalie, Ken Dryden. Boston was eliminated in a stunning first-round defeat as Montreal took the seventh and deciding game and went on to win the Cup.

The humiliation of losing the Stanley Cup did not last long. Boston ran all over the competition the next year, finishing 10 points ahead of New York and losing only 13 games all season. This time there were no slip-ups as Boston eliminated Montreal as payback for the previous season. Boston annihilated the competition the next year, losing only three of its 15 post-season games in taking a second Stanley Cup in three years.

The Bruins continued to place first or second in the league, but they never won another Cup. In another era the Bruins might have rung up six or seven Cups, especially with the talent they possessed. But Bobby Orr's knees couldn't hold up, and two other dynasties were reaching their peak at the same time: Montreal, with Dryden and Lafleur, and the rowdy Philadelphia Flyers. Nonetheless, Boston's hard work and tough defense signaled the beginning of a new era.

The Philadelphia Flyers: 1974-1975

They were known as the Broad Street Bullies, and for several years during the mid-1970s they swaggered and fought their way through the NHL. This team of tough guys was led by center Bobby Clarke and goalie

*The Flyer's Bobby Clarke gets after a Montreal Canadien.
The tough play of Philly's "Broad Street Bullies" made them
champions in 1974.*

Bernie Parent. Flyers head coach Fred Shero's motto
was: "If you can't beat 'em in the alley, you can't beat 'em
on the ice." No one ever played rough with the Flyers
and got away with it. In fact, their combination of
defense and fisticuffs made for one of the stingiest
defenses in the NHL.

In 1973-74, Parent played in 73 games, yet managed
to compile a sparkling 1.89 goals-against average with 12
shutouts—by far the best defensive performance that year.
As a result, Philly won the West Division by seven points
and went on to defeat Atlanta, New York, and Boston. In
the finals, the Flyers beat the Bruins handily, including a
1-0 shutout in the sixth and deciding game. It was the
first Stanley Cup for an expansion team.

In 1974-75, Philadelphia became the first Patrick Division champ in the newly-realigned league, tying Montreal for the league's best record with 113 points. In the Cup finals, the Flyers defeated Buffalo in six games for their second Cup (the first back-to-back winner since Montreal in 1968 and 1969). Bobby Clarke won the Hart Trophy as MVP for the second time in three years, while Parent won the Vezina and Conn Smythe prizes.

The Flyers won by intimidating their rivals, punishing the opposition, and scoring just enough to win. In the end, however, Philadelphia's dynastic plans were dashed, not by a tougher team, but by two teams who were faster and more stylish: the Montreal Canadiens and the New York Islanders.

The New York Islanders: 1979-1983

No team ever did what the New York Islanders did in so short a time. Created in 1972, it took the Islanders seven years to reach the Stanley Cup; afterward, it took the other NHL teams four years to unseat them.

Nothing came easy for the Islanders. In their first year, they lost seven of their top 20 NHL draft choices to the new World Hockey Association (WHA). In 1972, their record was 12 wins, 60 losses, and 6 ties. In their second season, they managed 19 wins. The only bright spot was that they earned great draft choices two years running. Their first pick was Denis Potvin. Later came Bryan Trottier and Bob Bourne; in 1977 they acquired John Tonelli and Mike Bossy. The acquisition of Bossy was the Islanders' greatest steal: Despite a brilliant record in junior hockey, Bossy was not at the top of any other club's draft list. Bossy turned out to be a franchise player, in the same way that Guy Lafleur and Bobby Orr had been franchise players.

After a shaky start in camp, Bossy became a scoring sensation, setting a rookie record for the most goals (53). Teammate Bryan Trottier's rookie exploits earned him a Calder Cup. He and Bossy were a perfect match on the ice. They seemed to have a telepathic ability to find each other and make great plays. On defense, Denis Potvin was nothing less than superb, and the slashing, checking style of goalie Billy Smith kept the crease clear of opponents.

The Islanders won their first division title in 1977-78, dethroning Philadelphia, but their inexperience in playoffs showed as they were defeated by Toronto. But by the following year, their scoring exploded; Trottier led the league in scoring with 144 points, while Bossy led in goals with 69. Trottier, Potvin, and Bobby Smith all took home individual honors, but the team was still denied a Cup.

The third time was the charm. Although they struggled through the 1979-80 season, the Islanders acquired Butch Goring from Los Angeles. With Goring in the lineup, the Islanders finished the season with a 12-game unbeaten streak. They finally won in the finals, beating Philadelphia in six games on Bobby Nystrom's overtime goal.

Once New York had learned the art of winning, they kept on doing it. In 1980-81 they not only finished first in the league (48-18-14), but sailed through the playoffs, beating Minnesota in five to take the Cup. In 1981-82, the Islanders won their third straight Cup in convincing fashion, losing only one playoff game. No one really expected the Islanders to pull off four Stanley Cups in a row. It had only been done twice before, both times by Montreal, and the league was in many respects far more competitive than in the Canadiens' era. The Islanders finished the regular season with 96 points—the worst finish ever for a Stanley Cup champion. But something happened on the way to the Stanley Cup. After they disposed of the New York

Rangers in the Patrick Division finals, the Islanders met Boston—the team that led the league during the season with 110 points—and beat them in six games. Finally, they met the Oilers and shut out Wayne Gretzky and Company in four games. But the Oilers were the new kids, and the following year would see the reign of a new Cup powerhouse.

The Edmonton Oilers: 1984-1988

No team has been so offensively dominating as the Edmonton Oilers. The Oilers were originally the Alberta Oilers of the old WHA. From 1972 through 1979 the Oilers stayed near the middle of their division until they made their greatest acquisition. His name was Wayne Gretzky, a 20-year-old center. In his first pro season, Gretzky burned up the WHA league with 46 goals and 64 assists. The Oilers finished first in 1978-79, but could not capture their first and last Avco Cup as Houston received that honor. The next year, the WHA folded and Edmonton skated off to the NHL.

Coach Glen Sather created a team strategy based upon the proven methods of the great hockey teams from the Soviet Union, emphasizing speed and stickhandling. In 1979, Sather selected defenseman Kevin Lowe, center/winger Mark Messier, and winger Glenn Anderson as his first three draft picks. All became superstars. In 1980, the Oilers drafted defenseman Paul Coffey and Finnish winger Jari Kurri. In 1981, they got goalie Grant Fuhr. Together with Gretzky, these players dominated the league for the next seven years.

In its first two years in the NHL, Edmonton finished fourth in the Smythe Division, while Gretzky, Messier, and Coffey developed into awesome offensive players. By the 1982-83 season, the Oilers were the league's powerhouse. They won their division with a

47-21-12 record, scoring 424 goals—90 goals ahead of their nearest competition. Coffey and Messier were two of the fastest skaters in the league. In Gretzky, they had the greatest all-time scorer and playmaker. In Kurri and Anderson, the Oilers had two of the league's best shotmakers. And with Fuhr and Andy Moog in the pipes, they could take chances on defense that other teams would never attempt.

The Oilers couldn't unseat the Islanders in 1983, but the next season they annihilated the competition, finishing 15 points ahead of Boston and New York. The Oilers established an all-time mark with 446 goals, a record 36 of them shorthanded. It didn't matter how many men the Oilers had on the ice, they always seemed to have the advantage. The Oilers cruised into the finals, requiring only the minimum 12 games to make it, and met the Islanders, who were driving for their fifth straight Cup. In the first game, the Oilers used a little of the Islanders' medicine, winning 1-0 behind Grant Fuhr's brilliant goalkeeping. The Islanders won the second game, but after that it was all Edmonton. With Gretzky and Messier leading the attack, the Oilers routed New York, 7-2, 7-2, and 5-2 for their first Stanley Cup.

The next season's victor was never in doubt. Jari Kurri finished the 1984-85 season with 71 goals, just two behind Gretzky. Paul Coffey collected 46 goals and 80 assists for another Norris Trophy. Mark Messier and Glenn Anderson pitched in 40-plus goals each. And Gretzky continued his march toward the Hall of Fame, scoring his 1,000th point. The result was another Oiler rout in the regular season, and a triumph over the Philadelphia Flyers in just five games.

Edmonton ran over everyone in 1985-86, registering a 56-17-7 record for 119 points, best in the league by nine points. It looked like another easy march

*Before he was traded to the L.A. Kings, Wayne "The Great One"
Gretzky led the amazing attack of the '80s Edmonton Oilers.*

to the Cup until they met an unlikely roadblock in the Calgary Flames. Tied 2-2 in the seventh game, Oilers' defenseman Steve Smith shot a goal into his own net to give Calgary the win. The Flames won the Stanley Cup in a most unlikely fashion. That mistake would not be repeated.

In 1986-87, the Oilers finished first in the league, and dispatched the Kings, Jets, and Red Wings in just 15 games to earn another shot at Philadelphia in the finals. They shot down the Flyers once again, winning in seven games for their third Cup.

The 1987-88 season would be the last winning year with The Great One. After mauling the Bruins in just four games (for their fourth Cup in five years), the Oilers' owner made the trade to end all trades. Gretzky, Mike Krushelnyski, and Marty McSorley were all traded (Coffey had been traded the year before). The very next season, the Oilers finished third in their division. They went nowhere except home after an early exit from the playoffs.

The next year started no better. Grant Fuhr went down with a shoulder injury and Andy Moog was traded. But the brash Oilers woke up in the playoffs and Mark Messier took up Gretzky's crown as the team leader. Edmonton met Boston in the finals. The first game was a classic, with the score tied 2-2 going into the third overtime before the Oilers' Petr Klima scored in overtime. The remaining games went to Edmonton, outscoring Boston 17-5 to take their fifth Cup in seven years. It was the last Cup for Edmonton. Glenn Anderson and Messier were traded, and the most talent-rich team in NHL history was no more.

The Pittsburgh Penguins: 1990-1992

From 1982 to 1988 the lowly Penguins finished no better than fifth in the Patrick Division. They found a silver lining in the 1984 draft, however, when they chose

Mario Lemieux of the Pittsburgh Penguins hoists hockey's greatest prize: the Stanley Cup.

Mario Lemieux. If one player can be called a franchise player, it's Lemieux. Other shrewd draft picks and trades brought a host of fine players: Mark Recchi, Rob Brown, Bob Errey, Kjell and Ulf Samuelsson, Tom Barrasso, Ron Francis, Bryan Trottier, Kevin Stevens, and Joe Mullen. By 1987-88, Lemieux had broken Wayne Gretzky's grip on the MVP and scoring honors. Later acquisitions of Paul Coffey, Joey Mullen, and center Jaromir Jagr of Czech made the Penguins a team to be reckoned with.

The outlook for 1990-91 dimmed when Lemieux needed back surgery. But Recchi scored 113 points, Stevens added 86, and goalie Barrasso performed ably. Somehow, the chemistry came together even without

Lemieux in the lineup, and Pittsburgh flourished. When a healthy Lemieux returned late in the season, Pittsburgh zoomed into the playoffs. They battled past New Jersey in seven games, beat Washington in five, then came back from two defeats to oust Boston in six before meeting Minnesota in the finals. They won the Cup in six games.

The next year, Pittsburgh became the power everyone thought they could be. Despite the sudden death of coach Bob Johnson, replacement coach Scotty Bowman led the team to victory. The Penguins beat Chicago in four straight games for their second consecutive title.

In 1992-93, Pittsburgh steamrolled over everyone. Once again, Lemieux saw limited action in 60 games, this time due to a form of cancer called Hodgkin's Disease. But even that wasn't enough to unseat him from his yearly position atop the scoring charts! Pittsburgh rambled past New Jersey in the first round, but met unexpected opposition from the Islanders in the Patrick Division finals. In seven hair-raising games New York unseated Pittsburgh, winning the seventh game, 4-3, in overtime.

Will Pittsburgh come back to win a third Stanley Cup in the '90s? With a healthy Mario Lemieux there is no doubt they could; without Lemieux, there is no telling. The Penguins remain one of the more powerful teams in the league, but there are other teams fighting for the top spot. Montreal, the 1992-93 Cup winner, has another classic team, featuring strong goaltending from Patrick Roy. But it takes more than one year to make a great team. It takes a whole string of them. If the past is any indication, it is only a matter of time before another team—often the team you least expect—emerges to become the next great franchise.

Most Stanley Cup Championships, 1892-1994

Teams	Years in NHL	Stanley Cups
Montreal Canadiens	67	24*
Toronto Maple Leafs	54	13
Detroit Red Wings	54	7
Boston Bruins	53	5
Edmonton Oilers	13	5

*Montreal won its first championship in 1915-16, two years before the creation of the NHL.

Best Winning Percentage, Single Season

Team	Season	W-L-T	Percentage
Boston Bruins	1929-30	380-5-1	.875
Montreal Canadiens	1943-44	38-5-7	.830
Montreal Canadiens	1976-77	60-8-12	.825
Montreal Canadiens	1977-78	59-10-11	.806
Montreal Canadiens	1944-45	38-8-4	.800

Most Goals, Single Season

Team	Season	Goals
Edmonton Oilers	1983-84	446
Edmonton Oilers	1985-86	426
Edmonton Oilers	1982-83	424

Most Wins, Single Season

Team	Season	Wins
Montreal Canadiens	1976-77	60
Montreal Canadiens	1977-78	59
Montreal Canadiens	1975-76	58

Glossary

BETWEEN THE PIPES. Refers to the area between the goal posts, otherwise known as the goal crease.

BLUE LINES. Two lines, one at each end of the rink, that are 60 feet from the goal line and define the attacking zone. They are also used to determine offsides.

CHECKING. Defending against or guarding an opponent. On a line, a right wing checks the other team's left wing, and a left wing check's the opposing right wing. Centers check each other.

FACE-OFF. The dropping of the puck between two opposing players to start play. Face-offs follow goals or other stoppages in action, and are to hockey what the jump ball is to basketball.

PLAY MAKER. Usually a center whose skating, puck-carrying, or passing abilities enable him to set up or make a play that can lead to a goal.

POWER PLAY. A manpower advantage resulting from a penalty to the opposing team.

SHORTHANDED. When a team is down one or two players due to a penalty; the defensive team on a power play.

STICKHANDLING. The art of controlling the puck with the stick.

Bibliography

Diamond, Dan & Joseph Romain. *Hockey Hall of Fame.* New York, NY: Doubleday, 1988.

Diamond, Dan, ed. *National Hockey League 75th Anniversary Commemorative Book.* Toronto, Canada: McClellan & Stewart, 1993.

Hollander, Zander, ed. *The Complete Encyclopedia of Hockey.* Detroit, MI: Visible Ink Press, 1993.

National Hockey League. *Official Guide & Record Book 1992-93.* Toronto, Canada: NHL Publications, 1993.

Sporting News. *The Sporting News. Sporting News Complete Hockey Book 1993-94.* St. Louis, MO: The Sporting News Publishing Co., 1993.

Photo Credits

Index